ON THE EDGE LEONID LERMAN

ON THE EDGE

The Sculpture of Leonid Lerman

Introduction by Michael P. Mezzatesta

Duke University Museum of Art
Durham 1988

This catalogue is published on the occasion of an exhibition at the Duke University Museum of Art,

Durham, North Carolina, September 9–October 23, 1988.

Copyright 1988   Duke University Museum of Art

Library of Congress Catalogue Card Number 88–706–86   ISBN 0–938989–02–2

Printed in U.S.A.   Design: Mary Mendell

Color photographs by Wendell Maruyama

Cover: *Volens-Nolens*, 1988. Painted terracotta 12.5 x 22 inches. Collection of the Artist

Frontispiece: *Self-portrait as Omelette*, 1987. Frying pan, cut and painted.

Private collection, New York.

CONTENTS

FOREWORD

Recent developments in the world of international relations may seem a distant concern to the everyday affairs of a university art museum. Yet, over the past several years the new policy of *glasnost* in the Soviet Union has resulted in a public debate affecting all aspects of Soviet society, especially the arts where works previously unpublished, unseen, or unperformed are now reaching a wide audience. For Americans, this openness has provided an opportunity to experience the extraordinary richness of a culture long in limbo as well as to understand something of the difficult history of a society where artistic expression has been subservient to political ideology.

Considering the interest that has been focused on the Soviet Union, the Duke University Museum of Art is pleased to open the fall season with an exhibition featuring the work of Leonid Lerman, a young Russian émigré sculptor trained in Odessa and Leningrad and, since 1980, a resident of the United States. The approximately 90 pieces in this exhibition have been produced over the last five years and include a wide variety of types and media— freestanding statues, reliefs, and assemblages made of wood, clay, and found objects, as well as a selection of drawings. His figuratively based sculpture—with sources ranging from ancient Greek art to Dada, Surrealism and Expressionism—present an ironic and highly personal view of the turmoil of life. Indeed, Lerman is often the subject of his own work as we can see in the amusing

Self-Portrait as Omelette (frontispiece) and in the numerous self-portraits in the exhibition. His sense of humor, at once satiric and playful, reveals a questioning mind probing the very essence of being. His images both delight and shock as he makes us think about the delicate nature of existence, perhaps nowhere more dramatically than in *Volens-Nolens*, the relief reproduced on the cover showing two men holding a razor blade aloft with their tongues.

As a Russian now residing in New York, Lerman has drawn inspiration from two worlds developing in the process a supranational perspective. His art offers a unique viewpoint not only on life in the Soviet Union and the United States but, more importantly, on the broader human issues that at once divide and unite two nations.

I am very grateful to Leonid Lerman for his help in presenting this selection of his work. Getting to know him was as great a pleasure as getting to know his art. His humor, energy, good sense, and inexhaustible supply of vodka made this a most memorable experience. I am also indebted to Abby Henig, his wife, who was so understanding and supportive throughout the course of the project. Hopefully, her screenplay recounting the amazing story of their Leningrad courtship will soon be produced. Special thanks must also be extended to the collectors who so graciously agreed to part with their works for this exhibition.

Through a fortunate set of circumstances, the Museum

was able to schedule at the last moment the show: Sergei L. Petrov—Moscow Photographs. This exhibition presents the work of Sergei Petrov, an artist currently living in Moscow. His extraordinary photographs provide a complementary vision to Leonid Lerman's sculpture. Mrs. Arthur A. Hartman, wife of the former Ambassador to the Soviet Union, was instrumental in helping to bring Mr. Petrov's work to Duke. We are very grateful to her and Ambassador Hartman for their assistance.

Michael P. Mezzatesta
Director

Figure 1 *Balanceada,* 1985. Terracotta, 8 x 5 ins.

INTRODUCTION

Dancing on the razor's edge, poised on one leg with arms outstretched and head thrown back—this is how we see the man in Leonid Lerman's small terracotta relief *Balanceada* (1985, Fig.1). It is, paradoxically, a dance of joy and anguish, of hope and fear—a balancing act for survival performed alone every day, day after day, in which good is pitted against evil. For Lerman, the razor is a kind of existential emblem on whose edge the struggle to exist occurs. Like the victim forced to dance by gun shots aimed at his feet, there is something tragicomic in the situation of man compelled to "dance" by events outside his control. Life on the edge, the subject of several sculptures, conveys the perilous equilibrium of existence—a central theme in Lerman's art. The struggle to understand life—to make art—is a solitary endeavor. There is an inherent loneliness in Lerman's work, a focus on the individual who, like the dancing man in *Balanceada*, must seek answers to questions without answers; who, battered by absurdity, must fight cynicism and romanticism as he walks the narrow path, the razor's edge. Through humor, satire, and especially irony, Lerman adopts a philosophical stance towards life's contradictory impulses in his constructed sculptures, reliefs, and ready-made assemblages and raises questions as he probes the roots of our existence.

For Lerman, whose own roots are set in two distinct cultures —Russian and American—this effort began in the Soviet Union and has continued in the United States.

He was born in Odessa in 1953 and educated at the Odessa School of Art and at the Professional School of Mosaics and Woodcarving before receiving his MFA in 1979 from the Mykhina College of Art and Design in Leningrad. Lerman's education in the Soviet Union represented the accumulated experience of many generations of Russian figurative sculptors and provided a solid training in the fundaments of his art. His education was also free. The sole condition was that he give back to the system what he had learned by perpetuating received traditions. It was the one condition he could not meet for it meant surrendering his artistic integrity. Like many artists in the Soviet Union, Lerman was unable to exhibit his work publicly outside of the authorized system of state-sponsored art, a system whose tenets of socialist realism demand stylistic and ideological conformity. The artist unwilling to embrace these standards could only function privately without hope of public recognition and with considerable risk of official disfavor. The anguish of being restricted in style and denied an audience—of being unable to express oneself—was acute. In that pre-*glasnost*, Olympic-boycott era, the prospects for a more open attitude toward the arts were extremely limited. After meeting Abby Henig in 1978, an American studying in Leningrad on an exchange program, the two were married and, in 1980, Lerman was allowed to depart for the United States.

When he arrived in New York, Lerman was, in effect, beginning from zero in a country whose language he

1

Figure 2 *Nude Youth Seated,* 1982
Clay, life-size

barely spoke and where he knew few Americans. Unlike
some other Russian artists, notably Komar and Melamid
who caused a sensation in 1976 at Ronald Feldman Fine
Arts in New York with their exhibition of "Sots Art,"[1] the
Soviet version of Pop Art, Lerman had produced no seri-
ous body of work in the Soviet Union as he left imme-
diately after graduating. Thus, he was faced with the task
of coping with a completely different world, one of which
he had no knowledge and in which everything was
possible.

In terms of American art, this meant a panorama
ranging from Conceptual and Neo-Expressionist to the
emerging Neo-Geo.[2] Not surprisingly, everything seemed
"strange and unacceptable." As he grew familiar with the

New York art scene, this initial rejection of his American
experience was followed by a rejection of his Russian
background—a dialectical process of growth and matura-
tion. Yet, ironically, before he could begin his own work
he had to use his skills just in order to survive. He worked
as a model maker for a jeweller; made reproductions for
the Metropolitan Museum of Art gift shop; served as a
private contractor specializing in the restoration of architectural ornaments; taught at the Sculpture Center Studios
in New York; and worked at the Johnson Atelier in Prince-
ton, New Jersey, one of the most technologically advanced
foundries in the United States. Here, the depth of Lerman's
formal training became apparent in the extraordinary
life-sized figure of a nude adolescent boy he modeled to
be cast in bronze for one of the Atelier's many commis-
sions (Fig.2). The delicacy and naturalness of the sculpture reveal not only the realism of 19th-century academic
art but also the refined idealism of the Italian Renaissance.
Although this statue was a swan song to the academic
manner, the human figure remains the central element in
his *oeuvre*—providing the key to understanding his art.

At the end of 1983, Lerman rented a studio on lower
Broadway. It was his first private work space, either in the
Soviet Union or the United States, and it meant that, for
the first time, he faced the task of giving form to his sen-
sations, or as he has said, "to collide with the world, . . .
to begin to see who you are." The fact that this moment
was delayed for four years does not mean that Lerman

was idle. Indeed, in the struggle to come to grips with the harsh realities of a new society where his talents were primarily of commercial interest, he was compelled to confront the American environment and to react to it with all its complexities and contradictions. The experience was emotionally and psychologically wrenching. When he arrived from Leningrad, one suitcase in hand, Lerman had to deal with the shock of the new and the confusion of a disoriented cultural identity. These four years were a difficult period that forced him to measure the American experience against his expectations as an émigré artist.

What has emerged in his art is not simply a reaction to a new life but to life in general. Lerman speaks to the absurdity of the human condition, to the trials and tribulations of every man, regardless of nationality. In this sense, Lerman's dual cultural citizenship allows him to cut across national differences and to focus on universal themes.

Bug City (1986) is one of the first sculptures seen upon entering the current exhibition (Fig.3). Its presence is startling for, although at seventy-two inches in length it is only slightly larger than the average New York City roach, it carries on its back a condensed version of the Manhattan

Figure 3   *Bug City*, 1986. Steel and wood, 72 x 43 x 25 ins.

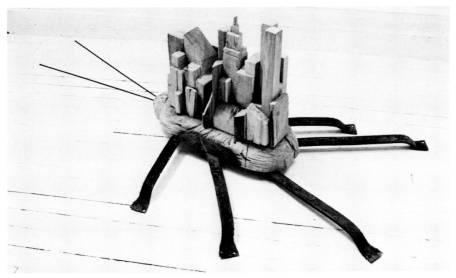

skyline. Like the Greco-Roman goddess Tyche who wears a walled image of the city as a crown to symbolise her urban domain, Lerman's *Bug City* stands, or perhaps we should say crawls, as a witty emblem of another kind of urban supremacy. Yet *Bug City* is more than a clever comment on the perils of living in New York. It is also a self-portrait. This Kafkaesque metamorphosis is doubly ironic. In the Soviet Union an artist working outside of the officially sanctioned state art organizations is liable to be branded a "parasite." In the United States, the artist's status is not threatened or, conversely, exalted by such a political-social stigmatization. Indeed, here the artist is likely to be but one of thousands anonymously struggling for attention—untested, unsure, unrecognized and alienated: pests, if not to the indifferent general public, then to the unfortunate gallery owners who have to deal with them. However worthless the emerging artist may feel, the emerging emigrant artist carries an additional burden for he also must cope with a foreign environment whose cultural weight bears as heavily as the skyscrapers in *Bug City*.

The first major works produced in Lerman's new studio confronted the artist's search for cultural identity. *Homage to de Kooning* (Cat.1) was inspired by *Acrobat*, a painting of ca. 1942. Although not unaware of American contemporary art while in the Soviet Union, Lerman effectively discovered a vast body of new material after arriving in the United States. De Kooning's early work had a particularly strong impact. The selection of this painting may seem a strange beginning for a sculptor trained in the classical traditions of modeling and carving, yet it was de Kooning's expressive freedom in his use of the figure—here beginning to be fragmented and abstracted—that was a source of inspiration. In the process of translating this image from two to three dimensions, Lerman developed the elements that characterize his work: a figurative based, constructed sculpture formed by the use of found and shaped raw wood; painted wood; modeled terracotta; mixed media and, most importantly, the division of the body into discrete components.

In Russia, Lerman wanted to make figurative sculpture that was perfectly finished and chased in meticulous detail, a work to stand in contrast to the grayness of everyday life. As he became familiar with contemporary artistic trends in New York, that goal was soon abandoned. His initial attraction to de Kooning may have been stimulated by the freedom of form and facture seen in *Acrobat* and assimilated in *Homage to de Kooning*. The carving of the wood torso, the texture of the plaster pants, the elegance of the fabric-wrapped figure at the upper left, and the brushstrokes of the painted background approximate de Kooning's handling of paint. This expressive treatment was carried further in *"See You Tomorrow,"* produced immediately afterwards (Cat.2). Against the backdrop of an old, painted metal door salvaged from the streets of Chelsea, Lerman has placed a crudely carved, wood figure mottled with arbitrary patches of white paint. In this free-standing relief, the rough, raw treatment and the unfinished quality stress the materiality of the wood and begins to define Lerman's aesthetic.

Journey Down Memory Lane (1984), was Lerman's first monumental, freestanding sculpture (Cat.3). It was particularly important as the artist's initial foray into what he has called "the human figure as battlefield." The source is the famous *Calf-Bearer* of ca. 575-550 BC in the Acropolis Museum, Athens (Fig.4). This work, cut below the knees and damaged on the right leg, has been completed in Lerman's statue with massive, schematically carved thighs and shins inspired by earlier types of Kouroi and by the addition of a second pair of hands at the waist. The Kouros' muscular torso with the delicate, vertical banding of drapery has been replaced by a heavy, split beam of wood. The effect is powerful. Its fragmentation, severe reduction of form, and concentration on head, hands and legs, convey the essential concepts of protection and heroic stasis.

To an artist trained in the realist, figurative tradition, this is an important accomplishment (cf. Fig 2), for Lerman pays homage to Greek sculpture even as he transcends its naturalism by developing an expressive strategy for dealing with the human form while retaining what he has called the "spiritual ecstasy" that Greek art embodies. Lerman has studied the classical figure so intently that it has become part of his subconscious motivation. If this

Figure 4   *Calf Bearer,* ca. 575–550 B.C.
Acropolis Museum, Athens

statue's truncated arms and wood-beam torso belie the archaic Greek source, the function of the figure as the vessel of meaning remains unchanged. The severed, reductive form of *Journey Down Memory Lane* and its evocation of the image of the good shepherd—one seen in Greek art, early Christian art, and in the sculpture of Picasso[3]—are both timeless and timely, ancient and modern, mediating a never-ending dialogue between man and himself, man and man, and man and the divine.

The personal element figures prominently in many of Lerman's early works. *Journey Down Memory Lane,* for

Figure 5 *Self-Portrait as Cicero* (detail), 1984. Wood and terracotta, 51 x 31 x 21 ins.

example, is autobiographical. The shepherd is a portrait of Lerman's first American friend, a colleague at the Johnson Atelier who helped him adapt to his new homeland. In *Self-Portrait as Cicero* (1984), the artist appears as the Roman statesman, philosopher, and orator (Fig.5). He is shown half-length, right hand grasping the podium, left arm thrown outward in an expansive, oratorical gesture, head crowned with laurel and tilted back in declamation. Yet the mouth is only drawn on the modelled clay head. The speaker cannot speak and, therefore, cannot be heard by his unseen audience. The eloquence of Cicero depended on language and rhetoric. Without such shared knowledge between speaker and audience neither the speaker's message nor artistry can be comprehended.

The complexity of Lerman's ideas may have exceeded his ability to express them in his new language, creating frustration in the face of his artistic ambitions. Yet his language is sculpture, his rhetoric is form. Despite being silent, the artist still speaks through the work itself.

Stranger in the Garden (1984, Cat.4), returns directly to a Russian source, Venedinct Erofeev's popular underground novel of the 1960's, *Moscow-Petushky*. Like George Orwell's *1984, Moscow-Petushky*, one of the most popular pieces of *samizdat* literature [self-published], was forbidden reading and so was circulated clandestinely.[4] This comic tale concerns the drinking adventures and misadventures of the protagonist as he travels on the train between Moscow and Petushky, a small town hours away.

The episode alluded to is the culmination of the book. After boarding the train, the hero, an inveterate drinker, exchanges cocktail recipes and vodka with his traveling companions until he passes out. He then has a horrible nightmare—the colossal statues, *The Worker and the Collective Farmer*, in the Moscow Fairgrounds park outside the Exhibition of Achievements of the People's Industry and Agriculture building, spring to life and begin chasing him (Fig.6). These statues—created for the Russian pavilion at the Paris Exposition of 1936/37—are extremely well known in the Soviet Union, occupying a symbolic status similar to the Statue of Liberty. They are the logo of Mosfilm, the most powerful Russian movie company, and appear before the opening credits slowly rotating toward the audience. Unlike the roaring lion of MGM, a corporate emblem of *Ars Gratia Artis*, the *Worker and the Collective Farmer* stands as a heroic symbol of "the people" united for the greater glory of the state. Widely used by official propaganda organs, this ubiquitous image permeates every aspect of daily life to the extent that it hardly can be escaped. Yet the gap between the group's message and reality have transformed its meaning, making it an emblem of state hypocrisy and the object of public cynicism.

These giant figures—socialist tools held high—pursue Erofeev's drunk in a comic chase across a dreamscape. Lerman's sculpture alludes to the nightmare's conclusion, the moment of capture. Reducing the figure to a block of wood with terracotta member and head, face grimacing

Figure 6 Vera Mukchina, *The Worker and the Collective Farmer,* 1936. Sheetmetal, colossal Moscow Fairgrounds Park

from the blows, Lerman visually rewrites Erofeev's story as the hero's intellect and manhood are "hammered and sickled." *Stranger in the Garden* is a national self-portrait—an allegory of Russian society escaping reality through alcohol. It is also a self-portrait and comment on the contradictions and absurdities that forced him to leave.

During the same year, the artist dealt with the other side of his cultural world. In September of 1984, Lerman and Vladimir Greigorovich, a Russian émigré friend, discovered an abandoned wooden boxcar in the middle of an undeveloped landfill in Liberty State Park, Jersey City,

Figure 7 Leonid Lerman and Vladimir Greigorovich, *Boxcar Metamorphosis*, 1984 (destroyed 1986)

across the Hudson River from Wall Street. Its isolation in a vast, untended open space and the spectacular view of lower Manhattan behind it and of Liberty Island to the south, inspired the artists to paint across the face of the boxcar the foreshortened shadow of the Statue of Liberty surrounded by scaffolding then being erected for its restoration (Fig.7). The red shadow was painted against a pink background—approximating the light of the setting sun— and was complemented on the opposite side of the boxcar by the shadow of the Empire State Building. When viewed from each side, both the Statue of Liberty and the Empire State Building were visible through the open boxcar doors, alluding to the shadow painted on the other side. This clever use of light and shadow at once dematerialized and rematerialized statue and building, extending them beyond their physical boundaries and making us marvel as we see them in a new way.[5]

The painting of a boxcar takes on a historical irony when we recall that during the Russian Revolution avantgarde artists painted railroad cars with propagandistic images and slogans hailing the cause of communism. Were it not for the obvious sincerity of the artists, the Shadow-of-Liberty boxcar might have been read as a Russian-American version of Sots Art—the exaltation of a popular political symbol to the level of parody. The fact that it escapes cliché is a function of the observer's patriotism and the artists' ingenious solution to the artistic

Figure 8 *Fantasy on 4th of July,* 1986. Terracotta, 14.5 x 5 x 3 ins.

challenge at hand. Lerman's stance, however, is more complicated in the terracotta statuette *Fantasy on 4th of July* of 1986 (Fig.8). In this later sculpture, unrelated to the boxcar-of-liberty, we see the progression in Lerman's work as he develops a symbology resonant of his personal experience. It is not an anti-liberty, anti-American, or anti-Russian statement. Rather this unexpected combination of two diametrically opposed symbols suggests the multiple levels of reality of an experience shorn of illusions. This work, and the related *FKNCTY,* (1986, Fig.9), grew out of what Lerman has called the "teasing

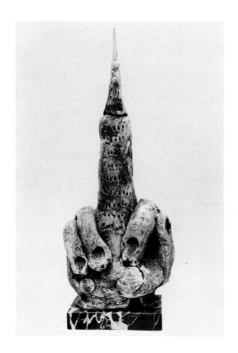

Figure 9 *FKNCTY,* 1986. Terracotta, 14 x 5 x 3 ins.

of ideas and materials" and ultimately stands without explanation.

Many of Lerman's works do, however, openly confront the problems of being an immigrant, acknowledging them as an essential part of his being. In the terracotta relief, *Death of an Immigrant* (1985, Fig.10), and the carved wood *Nightmare* (1986, Cat.5), a recumbent figure floats in mid-air with a Paris, Moscow and New York landmark at head, groin, and feet, recapitulating anatomically the melancholy history of émigré artists who have been forced to leave the generative source of their homeland. In *Bird's*

Eye View, the assemblage relief of 1985, a nude figure is viewed from above with arms and legs outstretched (Fig.11). The Twin Towers of the World Trade Center and the domes of the cathedral of Sts. Peter and Paul at his feet identify the sites as Manhattan and Rabbit Island, Leningrad. With one foot rooted in each culture and his arms pinioned by the clouds, this pathetic little figure is immobilized, spread-eagled—a prisoner of heaven and earth. His world is split. He suffers from an aesthetic, emotional, and cultural schizophrenia as he throws his Russian memories against American realities while searching for the hidden, metaphysical signs he believes to be present.

Lerman's self-deprecatory humor is seen in *Self-Portrait as Idiot* (1985–86, Cat.7), a twelve-foot high carved wood column of books extending from floor to ceiling in the midst of which is squeezed a large, forlorn terracotta head; in the precarious *Day of Sorrow* (1986–87), where a weary, stooped man is either buttressing or butting a tumbling skyscraper (Cat.8); and in *Cadmium Yellow* (1985), the colossal carved wood and terracotta man with an oversized yellow arm who, with a dull, dazed expression, calmly pokes himself in the eye (Colorplate 1).

Reflections or Symphony of Fingers (1985), presents two half-length figures with arms outstretched in the familiar American gesture of ill will (Cat.9). The spontaneous and vigorous expression of insult rendered and returned is heightened by the arm's length distance be-

Figure 10 *Death of an Immigrant,* 1985. Painted terracotta, 11 x 14 ins. Collection of Constantin Kuzminsky

Figure 11 *Bird's Eye View,* 1985. Lead, terracotta, wood stool, 22 x 15 x 13 ins.

tween the protagonists—any closer and the strong horizontal thrust of arms would be broken, any further apart, the compositional tension dissipated. Once more Lerman reduces form to the essentials—arms and heads. The clay heads, one dark the other light, are, in one sense, a "schizophrenic" portrait, an allusion to man's internal dialogue on life's endless choices. In a larger sense, they are accumulated portraits of the average man who, with a cool, stupid look, casually curses his neighbor. These dull faces convey the ennui of those inured by repeat performances of such digital symphonies but, perhaps more to the point, by the unrelenting complexities and absurdities of life. A work like *Reflections or Symphony of Fingers* strikes a sympathetic stance toward the subjects of the satire for, as the boat-base signals their mutual dependence, so their vacuous expressions should remind us that no action can be understood in isolation. This point is made directly in the terracotta relief *Twins* also of 1985 (Fig.12). Here the chain of nourishment moves upward from Romulus and Remus to the she-wolf; from the she-wolf to the wolf; and from the wolf beyond, recalling Lenin's dictum: "Everything is connected with everything else."

The painted terracotta reliefs of 1985 explore a variety of similar ideas. These small sculptures serve as three-dimensional drawings, often exploring themes related to larger works, such as the razor blade series (Cat.14-17). They are, in a way, modern day versions of Renaissance

Figure 12   *Twins*, 1985. Terracotta, 10 x 14 ins.

emblems — cryptic images whose meanings are not imme-diately apparent. The "Everyman" head appears in a series of these reliefs, smaller versions of the terracotta portraits on the sculptures discussed above (Cat. 19–30: Color-plates 2,3). Those heads are focal points, embodying the notion of the human and, in their material so easily broken, something of man's fragility. The same obser-vation pertains to the reliefs. The bathos of these ugly heads with large noses, big ears, and stubble beards is intentional — yet, despite their surreal situations and severed status, they have an integrity and innate dignity expressing the struggle to come to grips with simple human truths. The Breughelian reliefs, *Autumn, Spring* and *Summer* (Cat. 31–33), are the prototypes for the "Everyman" heads and ironical self-portraits. Lerman feels a deep affinity for Breughel's earthy images of peasants who, when eating, drinking, dancing, or pissing, capture the very essence of being and whose coarse faces bear the marks of life's trials on the most elemental level.

As Lerman's studio became filled with monumental sculptures, he began to work on a smaller scale. The change led to the development of new themes and types: a van Gogh series; found object tableaux; and assembled wall reliefs. In *Sower* (1986, Cat.37), Lerman combined elements from several van Gogh paintings in a surrealistic landscape dominated by the intense yellow sun and gnarled black tree. The title, of course, is taken from van Gogh's *The Sower* of 1888 with its Millet-inspired figure of a peasant sowing (Fig.13). Here, however, the peasant has been transformed into van Gogh's ear which sows as it walks (Cat.37, Fig.14)! The van Gogh portraits also offer a startling discovery when we realize that the artist's ear is actually a razor blade (Cat.38,39 and Colorplate 4). These moments of surprise, commemorating the most famous ear in the history of Western art, unleash a chain reaction of associations transforming the serene, pipe-smoking portrait of van Gogh into an image of the vision and anguish of artistic genius.

In this manipulation of levels of reality, Lerman reveals new layers of meaning. He does so as well by the juxta-position of everyday objects in new contexts. The dis-covery of a cache of pots and pans produced a number of found object tableaux. *Venezia, Journey Across the Grand Canal, Echo in the Valley of the Big Pots, Facing Eternity*, all of 1986 — appear against landscape or still-life back-grounds (Colorplates 5,6: Cat.64). The kitchen equipment becomes an integral, though incongruous, part of the tableau, creating a dada inspired scene whose meaning is hinted at by the miniature human figures. These simple objects can take on a higher, metaphysical status as the disassociation from their familiar context unlocks new expressive possiblities. In *Venezia* there is a playful metamorphosis as a spoon becomes a gondola, a pot top becomes a lagoon, and lead becomes water which itself merges with the water in the Canaletto painting in the background, creating an independent mini-world on the wall. A no less miraculous transformation occurs in *Self-Portrait as Omelette* (1987, frontispiece), where an ordinary frying pan has been cut into the portrait of the artist as fried egg, as Lerman has noted, with "knife and fork performing a ritual dance around the smiling victim who does not believe in death."

Figure 13 *Vincent van Gogh, Sower,* 1888.
Oil on canvas, Rijksmuseum, Amsterdam

Figure 14 *Sower,* 1986. Painted terracotta, 22 x 6 ins.

For Lerman, the simplest object holds the possibility for revelation. Readymade items presuppose the existence of a "meta-world" capable of access through irrational or even subconscious experience. Singled out for contemplation in isolation from its normal function, the large metal water pitcher in *Landscape with Figure* (1986, Cat. 40) is elevated to a higher plane. Its full body and sensuous form make it an emblem of ideal beauty while its water-carrying function suggests life-giving sustenance. Once again, Lerman surprises us—now with a conceptual reversal—when we discover the small figure of a man urinating on the base of the pitcher.

Still Life with Bird and Fruit (1987), continues Lerman's playful manipulation of reality (Cat.44). Here, a basket of fruit is set in a niche. However, the basket of fruit is not painted but is a photographic reproduction of an old master painting, cut out and glued to the background. Similarly, the niche is not a real architectural space but is fictive, coming from the same poster though overpainted in the upper area to enhance the illusion of depth. Cut out leaves and branches extend over the edge while metal tendrils curl up and into our space, continuing the twisting vines of the still life. "Painted" grapes piled before the basket tumble into the foreground as "real" grapes on the ledge. Lerman interweaves levels of reality as he plays games within the two-dimensional and between the two- and three-dimensional worlds. Mocking the Renaissance *paragone*—the controversy over the supremacy of painting or sculpture in the representation of nature—Lerman, expanding the boundaries of art as he plays, creates a hybrid artwork neither painted nor sculpted but composed of a poster and plastic fruit. This "anti-art" tableau is so "real" that it fools the bird who swoops in to pluck a grape. The allusion, of course, is to Pliny's famous anecdote of Zeuxis whose illusionistic grapes painted on a theater curtain appeared so life-like that birds flew down to peck at them. Here, however, the bird—though existing in real space—is made from metal, and pecks at artificial grapes, thereby completing the illusion and confounding both art and nature.

The mélange of the two- and three-dimensional continues in *Red Window* (1988, Cat.46). Foreground becomes window ledge on which actual cans of paint are placed. Through bright red mullions rendered in perspective, we look out to see almond tree branches in bloom. The background, a poster reproduction of van Gogh's painting, *Flowering Almond Tree Branches* in the Rijksmuseum, is brought into our space by the foreshortened frame, providing a "real" window into van Gogh's world. The bright yellow ledge, on which rest the wooden bottle with daffodil and the emptied cans of yellow paint, provides a transition between our world and that of art; between the materials of art and the process of their transformation. The intense, almost manic yellow of the ledge and the spent cans of yellow paint suggest a mind at once disturbed yet acute in its perception, one whose sensitivity to the world transmutes the mundane into the visionary.

The incorporation of ready-mades seen in *Red Window* is given a new twist in the *Scene of the Battle* (1988) and *Still Life with Paper* (1988) reliefs where vase, bottle, and knives allude to their man-made prototypes (Cat.47,48). However, the large-scale and hand-carved status—references to the monumental sculptures—set them apart. Nevertheless, as in the ready made tableaux, they assume an aura of the "meta-world." The effect, paradoxically, is to animate inanimate objects by giving them a life of their own. Each object contains a memory of things past as it recalls, in the shaped negative spaces within its form, a lost part of its essence. These still lifes, as well as *Sic Transit Gloria Mundi* (1988, Colorplate 7), establish duets within their individual elements alluding to the simultaneously complementary and contradictory relationships of objects and ideas, of thoughts and emotions.

Leonid Lerman's work is amazingly diverse in style, type, and media. As life is the criterion of his art, this is not surprising—for all things are susceptible to artful metamorphosis. As we have seen, Lerman plays with materials and objects, creating images whose juxtapositions generate new levels of meaning. The *Trumpet-Flags* —cut-out metal American flags joined to modifed brass instruments—offer silent fanfares (the horns are not playable) for their symbolic messages. To the circle of white stars on the flag entitled *Metamorphosis* (1988) have been added nine red stars, suggesting a hammer and sickle (Cat.49). On one level, this fusion could be read as an emblem of Lerman's personal cultural odyssey. Its ultimate meaning, rather, resides in the very act of its making—in the inspiration that melds flag and trumpet, hammer and sickle with stars and stripes, into a new sign which is more than the sum of its parts.

Perhaps the best way to characterize Leonid Lerman's work is to conclude with the recent *Moon Sonata* (1988, Colorplate 8). Here, Lerman has replaced the field of stars on the American flag with a detail of the heavens from *The Starry Night*—the haunting vision of the transfigured night sky in which van Gogh expressed his profound feelings toward nature, the infinite, the divine. *Moon Sonata* summarizes the essential aspect of Lerman's

art—the search for a higher truth—for *Moon Sonata* is, above all else, a symbol of the mystical, revelatory power of art.

Notes

All quotations to Leonid Lerman were from conversations with the artist on April 26, 27, and May 27, 1988

1. For a review of this exhibition, see Amy Newman, "The Celebrated Artists of the end of the Second Millenium A.D.", *Art News*, April, 1976, 43–46: Mare Fields, "Komar and Melamid and the Luxury of Style", Artforum, XVI, Jan.1978, 38–41. See also, Vitali Komar, *Komar/ Melamid, Two Soviet Dissident Artists*, (edited by Melvyn B. Nathanson with an introduction by Jack Burnham), Carbondale, 1979.

2. For a review of the art of the 1970's and 1980's, see H. H. Aarnason, *History of Modern Art*, New York, 1986, 560–690; Edward Lucie-Smith, *Art in the Seventies*, Ithaca, 1980; Howard N. Fox, *The Avant-garde in the 1980's*, Los Angeles County Museum of Art, 1987; Kim Levin, "Appropriating the Past: Neo-Expressionism, Neo-Primitivism, and the Revival of Abstraction," in *An American Renaissance: Painting and Sculpture Since 1940*, edited by Sam Hunter, New York, 1986, 215–224.

3. The shepherd with a lamb slung over his shoulders appeared frequently in early Christian sculpture, see *The Vatican Collections— The Papacy and Art*, The Metropolitan Museum of Art, New York, 1982, p.219, No.134. For Picasso's, *Man with Sheep*, see Roland Penrose, *The Sculpture of Picasso*, New York, 1967, 106–07.

4. On samizdat art, see *Russian Samizdat Art* (edited and with an introduction by Charles Doria), New York, 1986.

5. An inscription on the upper right corner of the boxcar read "Material Casts Shadows/Shadows Belong to Light." The boxcar was destroyed in 1986 as part of the renovation of Liberty State Park.

CATALOGUE

1 *Homage to de Kooning*, 1984. Wood, clay, fabric, plaster, 43 x 30 x 11 ins.

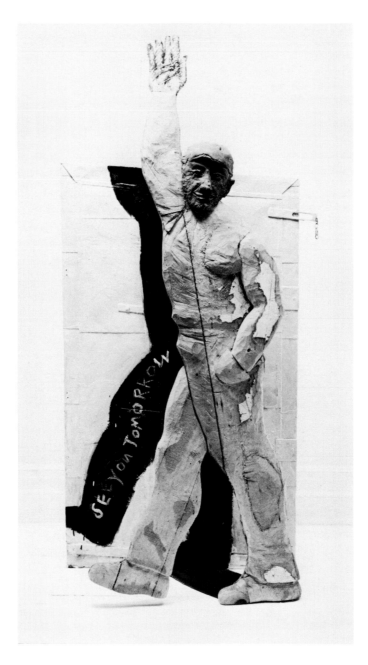

2 *"See You Tomorrow,"* 1984. Wood, clay, metal door, 85 x 39 x 9 ins.

3 *Journey Down Memory Lane*, 1984. Wood and terracotta,
81 x 25 x 24 ins. Private collection, New York

4 *Stranger in the Garden*, 1984. Wood, terracotta, and tin, 73 x 28 x 12 ins.

5 *Nightmare*, 1986. Wood, 24 x 89 x 2.5 ins.

6 *Fear and Trembling*, 1986. Wood, 33 x 12 x 5 ins.

7 *Self-Portrait as Idiot*, 1985–86. Wood and terracotta, 145 x 24 x 17 ins.

8 *Day of Sorrow*, 1987. Wood, 115.5 x 60 x 12 ins.

9 *Reflections or Symphony of Fingers*, 1985. Wood and terracotta, 77 x 31 x 12 ins.

10 *"Hello Leonid,"* 1984. Wood, terracotta and steel, 69 x 18 x 24 ins.

11 *Speak Memory. Speak Truth*, 1985. Wood, 71 x 25 x 25 ins.

12 *King of Beers*, 1985. Wood and aluminum, 22 x 8 x 7.5 ins.

13 *Big Swim*, 1986. Wood and lead, 7 x 16.5 x 23.5
Collection of David and Renee McKee, New York

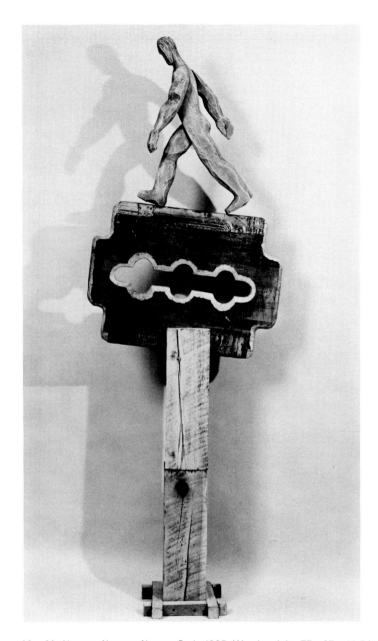

14 *My Narrow, Narrow, Narrow Path*, 1985. Wood and tin, 77 x 27 x 11.5 ins.

15 *Prodigal Son*, 1986. Wood, 16 x 6.5 x 4 ins.

16 *Boogaloo Down Broadway*, 1986–87. Wood and tin, 48 x 24 x 2.5 ins.

17   *Volens, Nolens, or Dream we Dream Together*, 1988. Wood, tin and nails, 37.5 x 20.5 x 3.5 ins.

18   *Me and My Brother in a Yellow Boat*, 1988. Wood, nails and lead, 51 x 26 x 9 ins.

19 *Nostalgia*, 1985. Painted terracotta, 10 x 15 ins.

20 *Man with the Open Mouth*, 1986. Terracotta, 15 x 10.5 ins.

21 *Death in a Restaurant*, 1985. Terracotta, 12 x 14 ins.

22 *Words Aren't Birds*, 1985. Terracotta, 10 x 14 ins.

23 *I Know What the Fish Told Me*, 1988. Painted terracotta, 16 x 11 ins.

24 *Bad Guy and Good Guy*, 1985. Terracotta, 12 x 15 ins.

25 *Boat with Two*, 1988. Painted terracotta, 10 x 12 ins.

26 *Tomorrow Is Gonna Be Rain*, 1988.
Painted terracotta, 10 x 16 ins.

27 *Pink Wind*, 1988. Painted terracotta, 9 x 15 ins.

29 *Morning Mirror*, 1988. Painted terracotta, 11 x 16 ins.

28 *Acrobat*, 1988. Painted terracotta,
12.5 x 11 ins.

30 *Last Wind*, 1988. Painted terracotta,
11 x 10.5 ins.

31 *Spring*, 1985. Terracotta, 8 x 10 ins.

32 *Summer*, 1985. Terracotta, 8 x 10 ins.

33 *Autumn*, 1985. Terracotta, 8 x 10 ins.

35 *A Long Time Ago*, 1986.
Terracotta, 9.5 x 11.5 ins.

34 *Man with a Stolen Leg*, 1985.
Terracotta, 10 x 14 ins.

36 *Spirit of the Road*, 1988.
Terracotta, 12 x 10 ins.

37 *Sower*, 1986. Mixed media, 50 x 25 x 16 ins.

38 *Self-Portrait as Vincent*, 1987. Tin and wire,
16 x 13 x 6 ins. Collection of Mr. Wade Thompson,
New York

39 *Self-Portrait as an Artist*, 1987.
Painted terracotta, 22 x 24 x 6 ins.

40   *Landscape with Figure*, 1986. Wood and found object, 26, x 13 x 15 ins.

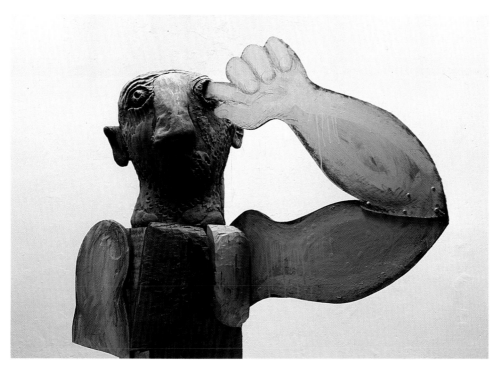

1 *Cadmium Yellow* (detail), 1985. Wood and terracotta, 84 x 47 x 20 ins.

2 *Voices*, 1988. Painted terracotta, 10 x 14 ins.

3 *Quarrel with a Cloud,* 1988. Painted terracotta, 15.5 x 10.5 ins.

4 *Portrait of the Artist or Vincent d'Arles,* 1987. Mixed media, 24 x 23 x 9 ins.
Collection of Mr. Wade Thompson, New York.

5 *Venezia, Journey Across the Grand Canal*, 1986. Mixed media, 15 x 10 x 8 ins.
Collection of Mr. Wade Thompson, New York.

6 *Echo in the Valley of the Big Pots,* 1986–87. Mixed media, 25 x 28 x 19 ins.

7 *Sic Transit Gloria Mundi,* 1988. Painted wood and nails, 32.5 x 52 x 14 ins.

8 *Moon Sonata,* 1988. Mixed media, 24 x 14 x 3 ins.

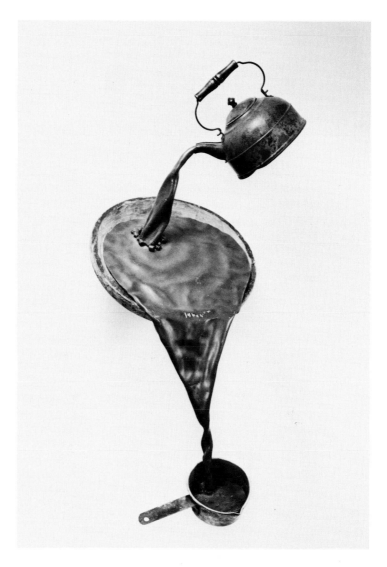

41 *Life of Waters*, 1984. Found objects, wood and lead, 39 x 17 x 12 ins.

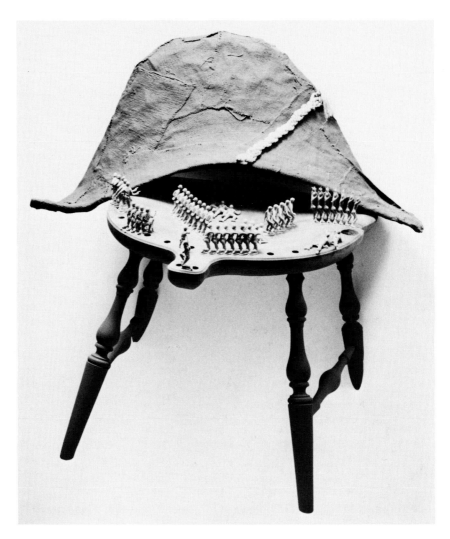

42 *Waterloo Chair*, 1988. Mixed media, 33.5 x 30.5 x 21 ins.

43 *Temptation*, 1987. Wood, 14 x 15 ins.

44 *Still Life with Bird and Fruit*, 1988. Mixed media, 33.5 x 30 x 9 ins.

45 *Red Divers, or Two Legs Are Better Than One*, 1988. Mixed media, 31 x 33 x 5 ins.

46 *Red Window*, 1988. Mixed media, 40 x 36 x 11.5 ins.

47 *Scene of the Battle*, 1987. Wood, 29 x 18 x 15 ins.

48 *Still Life with Paper*, 1987. Wood, metal and newspaper, 42 x 33 x 11 ins.

49 *Metamorphosis*, 1988. Mixed media, 26 x 16 x 3

50 *Untitled or Dark Eyes*, 1988. Mixed media, 34 x 12 x 3 ins.

APPENDIX

The following works are included in the exhibition but are not illustrated in the catalogue:

51. *Summer: Blue on Blue,* 1987. Wood and artificial flower, 27 x 12 x 6 ins.

52. *Spring Shower,* 1988. Mixed media, 24 x 20 x 5 ins.

53. *Serenade with Door Handle,* 1988. Mixed media, 30 x 12 x 3 ins.

54. *Deadly Loops* or *Music of the Spheres,* 1988. Found objects, 36 x 10.5 x 24 ins.

55. *Talking to a Wind,* 1988. Painted terracotta, 11 x 10.5 ins.

56. *Last Judgement,* 1988. Wood, tin and nails, 36 x 25 x 6 ins.

57. *Under a Cloud and Across the Sea,* 1988. Lead and clay, 22 x 10 x 9 ins.

58. *Lament,* 1988. Wood, terracotta and wire, 15 x 25 ins.

59. *Old Glory,* 1988. Acrylic on board, 42 x 42 ins.

60. *Morning Song,* 1988. Painted terracotta, 10.5 x 9.5 ins.

61. *One Glass Alive Better Than Three at the Funeral,* 1988. Painted terracotta, 10 x 9.5 ins.

62. *Last Water,* 1985. Terracotta, 14 x 9.5 ins.

63. *Words Are Not Birds. They Just Have Wings,* 1988. Wood, 84 x 15 x 6 ins.

64. *Facing Eternity,* 1986. Mixed media, 21 x 22 x 15 ins.

BIOGRAPHY AND REFERENCES

LEONID LERMAN

Born: Odessa. USSR, 1953

Professional Education

1965–1969	Odessa School of Art
1970–1971	Professional School of Mosaics & Wood Carving, Odessa, USSR
1974–1979	V.I. Mykhina College of Art & Design, Leningrad, USSR, M.F.A.

Selected Group Shows

1978	Menage Exhibition Hall, Leningrad, USSR
1982	Centre des Congres de Quebec, Canada
1983	"Terminal, New York", Brooklyn, New York
1984	Sculpture Center Gallery, New York
1984	Paulo Salvador Gallery, New York
1984	"Now" Gallery, New York
Jan., 1985	IMF, Washington, D.C.
Feb., 1985	P.S.1, New York
Feb., 1985	Galerie Marie-Therese, Paris
June, 1985	C.A.S.E. Museum of Russian Contemporary Art, Jersey City, NJ
July, 1985	"13 Hour Gallery", New York
Sept., 1985	Sculpture Center Gallery, New York
Nov., 1986	No-Se-No Gallery, New York
Jan., 1987	City Gallery, New York
Feb., 1987	Krain Club Gallery, New York
Apr., 1987	Kenkeleba Gallery, New York
March, 1988	Res Nova Gallery, New Orleans

One-Person Shows

Oct., 1985	C.A.S.E. Museum of Russian Contemporary Art, Jersey City, NJ
Jan., 1986	Paulo Salvador Gallery, New York
March, 1987	Tradition 3 Thousand Gallery, New York

References

C.A.S.E. Museum of Russian Contemporary Art in Exile, *Eight One Man Shows*, October 20-November 11, 1985.

Valery Gallery, *Cover Arts New York*. April 1987, 4.

Corrine Jennings. *In the Spirit of Wood*. Kenkeleba Gallery, April 5-May 3, 1987.

Dr. Nikolaj von Kreitor, "Leonid Lerman," *Cover Arts New York*, May 1987, 10.

Roger Green, "Nova Artists Shine Together," *The Times-Picayune*. March 6, 1988, 3.